Shared Pain and Sorrow

Reflections
of a
Secondary Sufferer

James I. Cook

The Pilgrim Press
New York

The scripture quotations are from the New Revised
Standard Version of the Bible, copyrighted © 1989 by
the Division of Christian Education of the National
Council of the Churches of Christ in the U.S.A., and
are used by permission.

ISBN 0-8298-0903-1

This book is printed on acid-free, recycled paper.

Printed in the United States of America
10 9 8 7 6 5 4 3 2 1

The Pilgrim Press, 475 Riverside Drive
New York, NY 10115.

"I Love Them Very Much"

The young girl in Chaim Potok's novel *Davita's Harp* is the child of a nonbelieving Jew from Poland and a nonbelieving Christian from Maine. She is thus denied the rich spiritual heritage of both parents. Her father and Jakob Daw, a close family friend in poor health, are correspondents in the thick of the brutality and bloodshed of the Spanish Civil War. Newspapers and newsreels in New York regularly assault Davita's hypersensitive soul with the horrible images of the war. Deathly afraid for both father and friend, she longs to pray but doesn't know what to say or to whom to say it. Finally she says simply, "Please protect my father and my Uncle Jakob. Please. Please. My name is Ilana Davita Chandal. Please protect them. I love them very much."

This is the confession of a secondary sufferer, the sufferer whose agony is born not of her own afflicted body or endangered life, but of the affliction and danger of someone deeply loved. What follows are the confessions of that kind of sufferer. For Ilana Davita Chandal, the primary sufferers were her father and her Uncle Jakob; for me, the primary sufferer was Paul, a nineteen-year-old son who battled

1

a terminal cancer for two and a half years. Because my confessions are responses to what happened, be warned that they may well be more personal than profound, more honest than orthodox. Some of them, I think, are very true; others may be less so. I set them down here, not because they are right or wrong, but because for me they simply *are*. Perhaps some part of them will also simply *be* for you.

Confessions About Prayer

From the moment of grim diagnosis and grimmer prognosis, intercessory prayer became a constant companion. In time, stammering petitions were joined by personal appropriations of Jesus' encounters with secondary sufferers. Mark 5:23 became "My son is at the point of death. Come and lay your hands on him, so that he may be made well, and live." Matthew 20:30-33 was reduced to "Lord, have mercy on us, Son of David! . . . Have mercy on us, Lord, Son of David! Lord, let our son be healed."

Within days of diagnosis, Paul's left leg was amputated two-thirds above the knee by specialists of the Mayo Clinic, and with that came an unexpected crisis. In the recovery room, for reasons that remain unknown, his

2

kidneys ceased to function. Accumulating fluids quickly put strain on the heart, and Paul was rushed to the coronary intensive care unit. For twenty-four hours he hovered between life and death without predictable outcome. During those hours the apostle's words to the Romans about prayer and the Spirit took on existential meaning. At times we really do not know how to pray as we ought. Because as long as there is life there is hope, I thought, ought I to pray that Paul live through this crisis? Or in the face of a future haunted by more surgeries and more suffering, ought I to pray that he be spared all that by a quick and comparatively easy death? I simply did not know, and so took refuge in "sighs too deep for words," trusting the Spirit to intercede with petitions I could neither find nor frame.

The Spirit prayed. Paul lived. My prayers returned to the feared progress of the deadly cancer. "O God, may the tumor removal have been in time. Let there be no metastasis to the lungs!" Within six months of the amputation, however, metastasis had occurred and demanded scheduling of the first of six lung surgeries over a two-year period.

As we settled into a heart-wrenching routine of CAT scans and surgeries in Rochester, Minnesota, of two- and three-week confine-

ments at St. Mary's Hospital, something began to happen to my prayers. Constant expo-
sure there to so many other primary and
secondary sufferers made it increasingly difficult to maintain a feeling of having been
singled out in some special way. Recurring
membership in the company of waiters outside the intensive care unit, a community that
gathered in early morning and parted in late
evening, pressed perspective on our anxiety
and grief. Every person in the waiting room
was a secondary sufferer. Each occupant was
linked by love to parent or spouse, daughter
or son, brother or sister, and prayed for their
recovery. Was there really any reason for God
to heed my prayers more than theirs? Did my
lifelong Christian faith, my ordination, my aca-
demic degrees merit special attention and ac-
tion from God? Had I the right to ask God to
save my sufferer while theirs wasted away
and died? And if God should do that, could
any of us stand my joy?

. . . About Healing

Slowly but surely such troubling questions
drove me back to Jesus' healing miracles.
There at last I thought I saw two things.
First, that Jesus' miracles had more to do
with the kingdom than with healing. The

health they brought to the sufferer and the joy they brought to the sufferer's family were gracious, personal, but secondary, gifts. Their primary and universal import was as signs of the kingdom, pointers to that promised reign when God will wipe away every tear from our eyes.

Death will be no more;
mourning and crying and pain will
be no more,
for the first things have passed away.
—Revelation 21:4

My second insight was that even in the days of Jesus' ministry, the people healed represented no more than a small fraction of the population. For every sufferer made whole, there must have been hundreds, perhaps thousands, left untouched. God has the power to heal, declares the New Testament, but it is silent on how the healed were chosen from among a sea of sufferers. These observations gently worked significant changes in my prayers. I now began to pray that God would choose to make Paul a sign of the kingdom. That choice, I saw, is always God's. In this century as in the first century the reason for healing this sufferer rather than that sufferer is ultimately locked within the secret of God's will. As a parent, I could do no less than

pray that by God's grace Paul would be num-
bered among the chosen, and promise that we
who loved him would gratefully witness to
that kingdom sign. But as only one member
of the vast community of secondary sufferers,
I could ask no more than that and still be
able to meet the red-rimmed eyes of my com-
panions. None of us could fault or praise the
other when the root of the miracle lay not in
the quality of our faith and life but in the
mysterious reality of God's grace. In the end,
I was to stand with the unnumbered company
of secondary sufferers whose primary sufferer
was not chosen to be that kind of sign of the
kingdom.

. . . About Life

In the years since, other confessions have
gradually taken form, confessions about life,
death, family, church, and God. I believe that
nothing trivializes what commonly passes for
life as instantly and lastingly as such crises.
Words that Lewis Smedes once used to pref-
ace a lecture on a very serious ethical issue
come to mind: "This morning," he said, "I
spent some hours for the first time with my
closest brother who a few days ago discovered
that he has a massive malignancy in his
brain. The problems of death and dying make

6

other problems seem fairly small." Indeed, but it is not only problems that are affected; the very stuff of daily life and work is suddenly declared irrelevant. I recall clearly my postsurgical returns from Rochester to the seminary classroom. How important was it to know whether the apostle Paul or a Paulinist wrote Ephesians? Did it really matter whether students could distinguish between the first and second aorist form of the Greek verb? Is the decision to record an A-minus or B-plus worth a second thought? Something in me wanted to shout that any such concerns were somewhere between secondary and silly. And yet, something else within me knew that that attitude was in part a reaction to the outrageous fact that although my world had suddenly come apart, the world itself went on. I had to come to terms with the reality that while we were sitting with Paul as he was prepped for still another early morning surgery, people all over Rochester, Minnesota, were beginning the day concerned about time, temperature, weak coffee, or burnt toast—just as I had done so many mornings while others sat where I now sat. The world did not stop when my world stopped, and I confess now that that is as helpful as it is hurtful. Work, structure, and routine can preserve sanity, do help us hang on, and may make the unbearable bearable. If my experience is in any way typical, many a secondary sufferer thanks God daily for the common tasks that demand both time and effort.

I also confess that such crises powerfully underline the preciousness of life and especially of its relationships. How much in life we take for granted. How much we fail to appreciate. How much we miss of life when we're content to participate on the surface rather than penetrate to the depths! The polite words regularly used to distance others from ourselves are rarely voiced in an intensive care waiting room, even among strangers. Secondary sufferers are mutually vulnerable and quickly move from brief introductions to gentle questions and quiet conversation about themselves and their primary sufferer. Persons with that experience inevitably agonize over why it takes catastrophe to connect us with each other at meaningful levels of either joy or grief. Few have expressed that tragedy more imaginatively and powerfully than Thornton Wilder in *Our Town*. Emily, dead for fourteen years, chooses to return home to relive what she remembers as a happy twelfth birthday. As predicted by Mrs. Gibbs, her cemetery companion, the experiment is disastrous. Death has made Emily so acutely aware of the brevity and preciousness of life that her mother's cheery breakfast chatter is unbearable. She begs her mother to look at her just once as if she really saw her. Total failure to work even the slightest change leads to the chilling climax of the play.

Emily suddenly realizes that she can't go on like this. Life is rushing past while she and the people she loves most are looking the other way. Devastated by the realization of how little notice she had taken of the incredible richness that each day held, she asks to return to the cemetery on the hill—but only after one last look at the world that had been hers. Through tears, she bids a wrenching farewell to Grovers Corners, to her parents, and to such ordinary, unappreciated things as clocks ticking, Mama's sunflowers, food, coffee, newly ironed dresses, hot baths, and sleeping and waking up. Abruptly, she turns to ask the Stage Manager if any human beings ever realize the minute-by-minute wonder of life while they are living it. Saints and poets, he replies, maybe they do some. So Emily returns to her grave, grieving over her discovery that that's all human beings are: just blind people! With some shame and much pain I confess to my share in this blindness and·pray for the miracle of sight.

. . . About Death

These confessions about life have been joined by two others about death. First, I know now that death and dying are not always the same thing, and that there can be a significant difference between the event of death and the process of dying. I know now that there are circumstances when even the mystery and finality of death—awful as they are—can be eclipsed by the clinical ravages of treatment and the unrelenting advance of pain. The initial blow comes with the dreadful realization that the common comforting phrases, "You're on the mend" or "The worst is over," no longer apply. Then treatment choices are not decisions between good and bad alternatives, but among only bad ones. Finally, incredibly, death itself actually becomes the best choice, and primary and secondary sufferer join to pray for the relief and release it alone confers.

And second, there is something special about the death of the young. Toward the end of his life, my primary sufferer managed to glimpse a sliver of light amid the gathering gloom. He was lucky to die young, he thought. People who live into their seventies or eighties often outlive family and friends. They may live out their lives terribly alone in the sterile anonymity of a nursing home peopled by changing shifts of strangers. How much better, he said, to face death surrounded by the people you love most! Grateful as I was that a primary sufferer could even think such thoughts, this secondary sufferer remains much nearer William Sloan Coffin's confession following the death of his son Alex:

> When parents die, as did my mother last month, they take with them a large portion of the past. But when children die, they take away the future as well. That is what makes the valley of the shadow of death seem so incredibly dark and unending. In a prideful way it would be easier to walk the valley alone, nobly, head high, instead of—as we must—marching as the latest recruit in the world's army of the bereaved.

. . . About Family

That parental insight serves to underline what I have come to confess gladly about the family: more than ever, I believe that family is a basic covenantal gift of God. That was certainly true of family in the sense of love between a mother and her child. From the beginning Paul knew that Jean would willingly have taken his cancer into her body, a simple fact that has left me in perpetual awe. Through every Mayo checkup, negative result, major surgery, and recuperative time, she waited and walked and willed with him. Devastated within, she exuded strength without for his sake. Then, during the home care of the last three months, haunted by twenty-four–hour morphine and oxygen, she never used her bed.

That was also true of family in the sense of love between a woman and a man. Ruth and Paul had been dating for a year before the cancer struck. Neither the amputation nor the terminal prognosis dimmed Ruth's commitment. Instead, before the year was out the two announced their engagement. At the time, given Paul's condition, that seemed to me an extraordinary but beautiful gesture. But admiration gave way to astonishment when, with eyes (and hearts) wide open, they decided to marry! The wedding was large, lovely, and festive, but what I remember most was hearing the familiar marriage vows "in sickness and in health . . . so long as you both shall live . . . to love and to cherish till death us do part" as if for the first time. The marriage was happy and promising, heartwarming in beauty and heartbreaking in brevity; above all, it was an unspeakably rich gift to Paul.

That their little family unit lived amid the larger family of parents and siblings was equally grace-full. Unforgettable assurance of that was Paul's final gift to us. Only days before death came, he secretly made an audiocassette on which, with remarkable humor and perception, he recorded his memories of significant family celebrations and characterized each family member. In one sense his words demand to be private; in another they deserve to be public, for it is difficult to imagine a more remarkable tribute to what family rites and relationships can mean to a primary sufferer.

. . . About the Church

If our family was able to be so much for Paul in his crisis, I confess it was in large measure due to the ways in which the church, "the household of God," ministered to us. More than one secondary sufferer has witnessed to me that it was experience with just such Christian pastoral care that taught them the full meaning of the confession "I believe in the holy catholic church, the communion of saints."

From the day of diagnosis we were the grateful recipients of pastoral care from Christians beyond numbering. Our local church, the seminary community, and the larger church lavished love upon us.

From our own community we received this message:

I wish I had the skill to speak the word that would really bring comfort to you and your family, especially to Jean and Ruth who have those highly specialized relationships of mother and wife. All I can do is assure you that we do care and our caring is only a dim, very dim indeed, reflection of the way our Lord cares.

From the West Coast:

We don't pretend to have any insights that you don't have, but only want to say that we love you.

From the East Coast:

I have no great words to convey, no scripture passages to quote, no consoling comments. As in all things like these, I am silent before what seems to me to be the silence of God. Mostly I want to rage, and perhaps that is the most honest emotion I have. But I want you to know that my heart breaks with you and my prayers (both the rage and for grace) are for you.

And from abroad:

This is just a very short note to say to you and Jean and all of you that Ruth and I so feel for you in the terribly hard days you are having to go through and we pray for you. Only the living and faithful God can give us the comfort and strength we need in all our distresses, but he certainly can do so and will. We shall often remember Paul and you in our prayers.

The outpouring of words and deeds was so massive that I desperately wanted to respond at the memorial service. At the same time there was genuine fear that I might go to pieces emotionally in the attempt. Therefore, no hint of my participation appeared in the Order of Worship. At one point in the service, the pastor was to look at me in the pew, and I would either shake my head or rise and come forward. My grateful confession is that the moment I entered the church, I knew it would be all right. Around me were the people of God from whom I had drawn strength for two and a half years. We were gathered in the place where through the years God had met us and our children in Word and Sacrament, where we regularly confessed through hymn and creed our belief in "the resurrection of the body, and the life everlasting." Little wonder that in those moments the grace of God and the communion of saints joined forces to give strength for words of testimony and of thanks.

. . . About Faith

Finally, this secondary sufferer reaffirms his faith in God. I say this at the end because of its importance; I say this at all because it is never a confession to be assumed. In the depths of their agony, most sufferers, primary or secondary, may be driven to embrace the biblical advice "Curse God, and die [Job 2:9]" or join in the little song from Archibald MacLeish's *J.B.*:

> If God is God He is not good,
> If God is good He is not God.

In those moments, the words of Henry Slonimsky ring true: "The assertion of God in a godless world is the supreme act of religion." By God's grace, Christians go on to assert that "God is for us" even in the midst of tribulation, distress, persecution, famine, nakedness, or sword.

It is not because I understand why such unspeakable things happen in a world where God reigns that I stand with those who believe. *Why*, in fact, was never my question, simply because I could not then and cannot now conceive of any explanation which would make me think that what happened was somehow all right. That is not to deny that some good and beautiful experiences came to our son and his secondary sufferers in the course of grief. They did come and were so moving that I never sing "sorrow and love flow mingled down" or "did e'er such love and sorrow meet" without thinking of our ordeal. That here and there, now and then, it was possible to trace some rainbows through the rain surely made holding onto God a bit easier. But what ultimately made trust in God's goodness possible, in the face of so much evidence to the contrary, was the cross. There at the center of the gospel lie mixed together the wonder of love, the horror of evil, and the mystery of undeserved suffering and death. Each of these realities exceeds my grasp, but each of them is also an eloquent witness to the deepest of all realities for sufferers: in ways and for reasons beyond our knowing, God is not outside the worst that happens to us, but fully in it with us. To that God I cling—and by that God I am held—confessing with gratitude and joy that nothing in all creation will ever be able to separate even sufferers from the in-Christ-Jesus-love of God!

A Pair of Pastoral Postscripts

My first postscript is addressed to the community of faith. After the long, drawn-out illness and death of his wife, C. S. Lewis (writing under the name of N. W. Clerk) poured out his deep sense of loss on the pages of a little book entitled *A Grief Observed*. One paragraph touches with particular poignancy on a common problem faced by all who wonder what to do or say (or what not to do or say) upon meeting a sufferer trailing clouds of sorrow.

> An odd by-product of my loss is that I'm aware of being an embarrassment to everyone I meet. At work, at the club, in the street, I see people, as they approach me, trying to make up their minds whether they'll "say something about it" or not. I hate it if they do, and if they don't. Some funk it altogether. R. has been avoiding me for a week. I like best the well brought-up young men, almost boys, who walk up to me as if I were a dentist, turn very red, get it over, and then edge away to the bar as quickly as they decently can. Perhaps the bereaved ought to be isolated in special settlements like lepers.

I confess that my experience differs at only two points. I never hated it if people chose to say something about Paul's death. And, except in unusual circumstances, Lewis' final suggestion about isolating the bereaved must be taken as a painful counsel of despair or disappointment. The bereaved neither desire nor deserve the added agony of isolation under a stigma of grief. But for the rest, Lewis speaks for all sufferers, both primary and secondary. Members of the community of faith will greet the sufferer warmly and ought to say something about whatever loss is being mourned. Sufferers who find it too painful to talk about their grief will say so, but others should not presume to know that in advance. Whatever its nature, their tragedy is the most important reality in their lives. It eclipses everything else, and more often than not they both want and need to tell their story. Very possibly, somewhere in the telling the voice will break and tears will flow. Remember that nothing is more natural than such weeping and that few things will prove more helpful or healing, especially if the comforter responds with touch or hug. At such moments, words are neither wise nor welcome. Presence, listening, touching, embracing, and the sympathetic tear communicate more than can be spoken. Compassion and love bring a ministry that often passes understanding.

My second postscript is addressed to the community of sufferers. It begins with a plea to make every effort to keep yourselves available to the community of faith. That community needs to offer ministry as much as you need to receive it. Inevitably, the first Sunday after your loss presents a crisis. Should you attend church or not? Will the congregation be comfortable with your presence? Will you be comfortable with theirs? The wise sufferer will finally set all such questions aside and simply go. That sanctuary is the place where the gospel of the resurrection is proclaimed in Word and Sacrament, and where the reality of the communion of the saints is both confessed and experienced. Fellow Christians welcome the opportunity to express their love and to help carry your burden. You need to let the tie that binds your hearts and minds in Christian love work its blessing on you both.

Know also that as time goes on there may be both painful and pastoral moments in your grief. The loss, the emptiness, the separation will subside to a dull ache you learn to live with. But that dull ache will be painfully interrupted now and again as you stumble, at unexpected moments, into little ambushes of grief. Confronting her remarkable look-alike in a restaurant, glimpsing his familiar make and model automobile on the street, or passing the departure gate for Rochester, Minnesota, in the airport concourse can trigger an instinctive response of love or memory followed by an anguished return to the devastating reality, all in a fraction of a second. Sometimes nostalgically, sometimes cruelly, the pain lingers on.

Yet your experiences with grief can also bring you opportunities for pastoral care. A few months after Paul's death, the orthopedic surgeon who had diagnosed his illness telephoned to ask if I could come to the hospital to meet a couple and their twelve-year-old son. They and their son had just been told that he had osteogenic sarcoma. I went at once, grateful to God that as other sufferers had reached out to me, I could now reach out to them. These sufferers and I had never met, but without hesitation we put our arms around one another, held one another, and wept. It was painfully easy for me to identify with their feelings, for my own experience with grief had prepared the way. As nothing else can, suffering, whether primary or secondary, enables us to fulfill the apostolic word to weep with those who weep and to comfort those who are in any affliction.